RALLY!
A Reading Program

Level C

Nature's Mysteries
Today and Tomorrow
Open Doors
In New Directions

RALLY!

A Reading Program

Sandra McCandless Simons

Nature's Mysteries

HARCOURT BRACE JOVANOVICH, PUBLISHERS

Orlando New York Chicago Atlanta Dallas

Sandra Simons taught reading at the junior high school level in Pacifica, California, from 1967 to 1973. During those years, she developed and used practical strategies for teaching reading in the classroom. In 1973 she began working as a learning disability teacher in California's program for educationally handicapped children.

Consulting Specialists in Reading

Eileen Bowles
Language Skills Teacher
The School District of Philadelphia
Philadelphia, Pennsylvania

Dorothy Jensen
Teacher
Laguna Salada School District
Pacifica, California

Eli Wucinich
Reading Coordinator
Thunderbird High School
Glendale Union High School District
Glendale, Arizona

Printed in the United States of America   ISBN 0-15-338117-5

Photographic Research Credits: The Bettmann Archive: 3, 117; UPI-Compix: 7, 29; Brown Brothers: 9; Wide World Photos: 27; Historical Picture Service: 28, 114; Dr. Ronald H. Cohn, The Gorilla Foundation, Menlo Park, California: 33, 57, 58, 60, 61; Paul Fusco, Magnum: 38, 45, 46, 47, 62, 63, 64; Carl Roessler: 99, 122; Jeff Foott, Bruce Coleman Inc.: 105; Marc Webber: 106; Department of the Navy, Navy Oceans Systems Center, Hawaii Laboratory, Kailua: 112, 127; Culver Pictures Inc.: 113; Sir Peter Scott, photo by Photo Trends: 115; Dr. Beatrice Gardner, University of Nevada: 35, 37, 39, 40, 41, 42, 43; Photographed by the Academy of Applied Science, Photo Trends: 116; Larry Ford, Scripps Aquarium-Museum: 123.

Art Acknowledgments: Kazuhiko Sano: 1, 4, 5, 6, 8, 10-11, 12, 13, 14, 15, 16-17, 18, 19, 20, 21, 22-23, 24, 25, 26, 30; Karl Edwards: 44, 48, 49, 50, 52; Jaclyne Scardova: 65, 67, 68-69, 70-71, 72, 73, 74-75, 77, 78, 79, 81, 82, 83, 84-85, 86-87, 88, 89, 90-91, 92, 93, 94-95, 96; Randy Berrett: 97, 100-101, 102-103, 104, 107, 108-109, 110, 111, 118-119, 120-121, 125, 126, 128.

Cover Credit: Kazuhiko Sano.

Copyrighted Photos: Dave Bartruff © 1979: 31, 32.

Contents

Nature's Mysteries

Disaster in Tokyo

In 1923 an earthquake rocked Tokyo. The fire that followed destroyed a large part of the city. This is the story of that disaster and of two people who lived through it.

1

The First of September

In the Japanese tradition the first day of September is a day to watch out for. It is a day likely to bring a storm or an accident or something else dangerous. But on September 1, 1923 the sun came up bright and strong in the city of Tokyo, Japan. No one really expected anything bad to happen that day. It was warm and clear. It looked as if it would be a fine day.

People started making plans for the weekend. Many people were already leaving the city. They were looking forward to two days at the beach. The platform at the train station was crowded. Some people carried large straw baskets filled with food and beach clothes. They talked and laughed as they waited for the train.

One person who was planning a weekend trip was a 12-year-old girl. Her name was Makiko Aoki. She was going to take the afternoon train to Oiso, a beach resort. Her mother was already there, waiting for her. Makiko wrapped her clothes up in a beach towel. She put on her new dress. She could hardly wait to go.

Other people were still at work. In his clinic
Dr. Eikichi Ikeguchi was treating the last patient of
the morning. When Dr. Ikeguchi had finished caring
for his patient, he would go home for lunch. He
lived near the Sumida River, not far from Makiko's
house.

As noon came closer, men and women all over
the city started getting ready for the midday meal.
Many people went down to the river to get water
for cooking. In each house rice would be boiled on
a small coal stove. The stove stood in the center
of the main room. Meat or fish would be added to
the rice. At noon lunch would be ready.

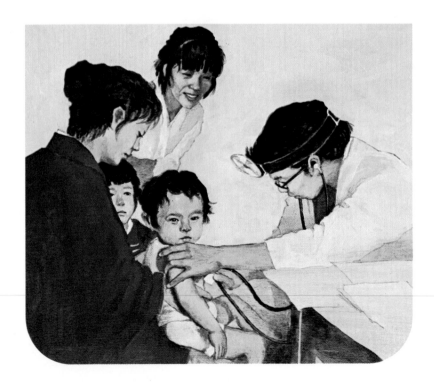

While the city people enjoyed the fine day, people in the country outside Tokyo were noticing some strange things. The clear lakes and springs had become muddy and warm. Animals on farms were acting oddly. Horses kicked the walls of their stalls as if they were afraid of something. Birds hopped from tree to tree, not flying, calling loudly.

The dogs, too, were upset. They cried and barked all morning. It was as if they sensed an enemy nearby that no one else could see.

2

Earthquake and Fire

At two minutes before noon the ground in the city of Tokyo suddenly shook with a terrible force. Again and again the earth rumbled and bucked. All over Tokyo buildings tumbled. The hill above the train station shook and split. A landslide roared down toward the platform. It swept down a cliff and into the sea. The falling earth took the station, the train, and 800 people with it.

Makiko was in her room when the earthquake hit. She felt the whole house shake and rattle. Right away she crawled under her desk. If the roof should fall, the desk would protect her. When the first shock was over, she grabbed her chair and held it over her head. She ran to the kitchen. Here she found her grandmother, her grandfather, her uncle, and her brother. For a while they all stayed there. The house kept on shaking for a long time. At last Makiko's uncle went up on the roof to look out over the city. In the distance he saw smoke. When he came back down, he told the family that he thought some houses were burning.

What Makiko's uncle thought was true. In thousands of small paper and wood houses the coal stoves tipped over when the earthquake hit. The hot coals set the straw floors on fire. In seconds the houses were in flames.

The fire spread fast. In half an hour the city was burning. Even on the Sumida River a fire was raging. Oil had leaked from hundreds of small boats. The burning oil had turned the Sumida into a ribbon of flame.

People crowded along both banks of the river, running toward the bridges. They were trying to get away from the fire. They thought that the other side of the river would be safer. They didn't know that the city was burning on both sides of the river.

The people crowded onto the bridges. They carried their clothes and their bedding with them. Sparks from the fire fell on the cloth that they carried. The cloth began to burn. Soon the bridges, too, were on fire. Four of the Sumida's five bridges fell in flames. On the fifth bridge a police officer wouldn't allow people to carry things with them. By doing this he saved the bridge and the lives of thousands of people.

As the afternoon went by, clouds began to form over the city. People hoped rain might be on the way. The clouds were really smoke. The day became almost as dark as night. Bits of burning wood flew through the air. Near the earth the sky was red—a sunset of fire.

The fire rushed through the city. The red-hot air mixed with colder air and caused tornadoes to form. Often a tornado is a tall column of whirling wind. These tornadoes were columns of fire. They roared through the streets. Houses were smashed. Doors, trees, cars, and people were tossed high into the air.

Some people tried to escape by getting to the sea. But the beaches were no safer than the city. The earthquake had caused a great tidal wave. Walls of water rushed toward the shore. They carried fishing boats far inland. They flattened hundreds of houses and dragged them out to sea.

Dr. Ikeguchi's house hadn't been harmed by the earthquake. For several hours he had stayed there. He treated dozens of injured people who showed up at his door. He saw that the fire was heading his way. But he stayed to take care of as many people as he could. At last the flames came right up to his house. It was time to go.

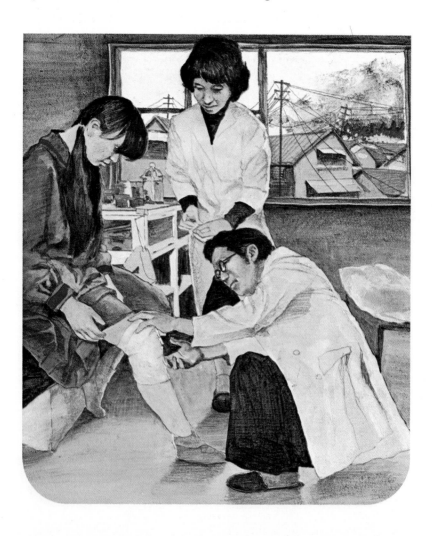

3

Eikichi Ikeguchi's Story

Dr. Ikeguchi bundled his family into a wagon as
fast as he could. Quickly they headed away from
the fire. They went to the house of some friends,
the Yasudas. The Yasudas lived in a large brick
house. The house stood in the center of a huge
garden. When the Ikeguchi family arrived, they saw
that other families were there, too. They had come
to the Yasudas' garden to escape the flames. In
an hour 60 families were in the garden. They were
talking, eating, and moving around. To the children
it seemed like a picnic.

Then suddenly, with a roar like a jet engine, a tornado hit the garden. Flames began to whip through the trees. A hot wind hit people like a wall. Screaming, people ran for cover.

At the side of the Yasudas' house was a long covered walkway. It led from the garden down to the river. It was like a tunnel. People swarmed into it, hoping to get away from the fire. Dr. Ikeguchi carried his two older children. Mrs. Ikeguchi strapped the baby to her back. Stumbling and bumping against other people, they ran toward the end of the tunnel.

The tunnel had become a trap. The wind blew the fire straight into it from the garden. At the other end a car blew up and became a ball of flame. The fire was now coming in both ends of the tunnel. The people were trapped.

Dr. Ikeguchi stopped running. He stood still in the tunnel with his wife and three children. All around them people screamed and cried. A red-hot wind filled the tunnel. Dr. Ikeguchi closed his eyes and waited to die.

Seconds passed. All at once it became very quiet. Dr. Ikeguchi opened his eyes. He was the only person left standing in the tunnel. Everyone else lay very still. He saw that his wife and three children were dead. For a moment he, too, wished to die.

Most likely his alpaca jacket had saved his life. It hadn't burned. Even so Dr. Ikeguchi was badly burned over much of his body. He could hardly breathe. But he made up his mind that he must try to save himself. Slowly he crawled out of the tunnel. He came to a tree with loose earth around its roots. He put his face in the cool earth and breathed through it. Then he crawled on.

After a long time he found his way to the river. It was no longer on fire. He found a small boat partly filled with water and pulled himself into it. In the water his burns were less painful.

It was five days before help came for Dr. Ikeguchi. By that time he couldn't walk or move. At last someone found him and took him to a shelter for injured people. Slowly he recovered from his burns. But the memory of that terrible day will always be with him.

4
Makiko Aoki's Story

At Makiko's house, the Aoki family was talking about what they should do. They couldn't stay where they were. The fire was heading toward them. At last they decided that they would be safest in a large, open space. There the fire would have nothing to burn. Not far away there was a place where several large buildings had been torn down. These buildings had been the army clothing depot. The buildings were no longer there, but people still called the empty place the army clothing depot. This was where the Aoki family decided to go.

Makiko already had her clothes wrapped up in her towel, so she set out first. She agreed to wait by the entrance to the clothing depot. There her family would be able to find her.

Normally the walk from Makiko's house to the depot took about ten minutes. That afternoon it took an hour. The streets were clogged with hundreds of people. Rubble from the earthquake also blocked many streets. When Makiko finally arrived, she found a large crowd already there. Her family would never find her. So she tied her beach towel to a long stick and held it in the air. It was like a sign to her family saying, "Here I am!"

Time went by. The large, empty space became filled with thousands of people. Families sat together on straw mats. People were talking, eating lunch, or napping. Most people knew that their houses would be burned down. They knew that they would have to wait here until the fire burned itself out. They didn't think that they were in any danger.

After a while the sky began to grow dark with smoke. Booming noises sounded in the distance. Suddenly Makiko felt a shock. Flakes of fire began falling everywhere. The people all around her began to run. They didn't know what they were running from or where they should go. There was no room to move. People fell over each other in great piles.

Makiko ran, fell, and fainted. Minutes later she awoke, staggered to her feet, and ran again. She gasped for air. Smoke and fire were everywhere. She kept running, falling, fainting, and running again. Finally she reached a pond. There she stepped quickly into the water.

Much later Makiko found her grandmother, her father, and her brother. They were unharmed. The Aoki family had been lucky. The tornado of fire that swept the army clothing depot had killed 40,000 people.

5

Afterward

The Great Tokyo Earthquake caused the biggest fire the world has ever seen. Together the earthquake and fire killed 140,000 people. Most of the city of Tokyo was destroyed.

In the first few days after the earthquake the city was in total disorder. Thousands of people roamed the streets looking for their families. There was no food or water.

At last help began to arrive. Doctors and nurses came from all over Japan to treat the people who were hurt. Shelters made out of rubble and old army tents were built in the burned-out parks. Doors were used for roofs and blankets for walls. At the shelters people stood in long lines to get warm food and medicine.

When news of the Tokyo earthquake went out to other countries, money flowed in from everywhere. The money helped to rebuild roads and bridges. It put many people back to work.

Slowly people began putting their city and their lives back together. Fishers fixed their boats and went back to sea. Shopkeepers sold what they had left at low prices and started over. City workers repaired water mains and fixed power lines.

As people worked to rebuild the city, they came to feel very close to one another. The disaster had brought them together. Some people even felt strangely happy. Everyone wanted to treat others with kindness, to work hard, to make a fresh start.

They also wanted to guard against the same kind of disaster happening again. A special school was started in Tokyo to study earthquakes. Today the scientists at the school tell people in other countries what to do when an earthquake hits. The scientists are also learning how to tell when an earthquake will happen. They take their clues from nature. They watch the weather, the trees, and the animals closely.

In time scientists around the world may be able to tell just when an earthquake is going to hit. Of course, no one can keep an earthquake from happening. But if people have warning, they can be ready. They can stay in safe places and be careful with fire. They can have emergency supplies on hand. They can make sure that what happened in Tokyo in 1923 will not happen again.

Animal Talk

Can people communicate with animals? Some scientists say yes. To prove it, they will introduce you to chimps that use sign language and have conversations with computers.

1

Talking Animals

Washoe could use 132 words by the time she was five years old. She could ask for things she wanted. She could name things she saw in pictures. She could tell people how she felt.

This may not seem surprising. Most five-year-old children can use many more words than Washoe could. But Washoe isn't a child. She is a chimpanzee.

Many animals can understand words they hear, of course. Even dogs understand a few. But dogs can't answer in words. They can learn to do what they are asked to do. Anyone who has a dog knows that dogs can show people how they feel. They can't carry on conversations, however. They can't put words together to form sentences.

Washoe was the first animal to learn a human language. Of course, Washoe can't speak. Chimpanzees aren't able to talk. The shape of their mouths and throats makes it hard for them to form words.

Before the 1960s scientists tried to teach apes words by shaping the apes' mouths as they made sounds. Only a few apes came close to speaking. Scientists thought that apes were not intelligent enough to learn words. Now scientists are finding that this idea isn't true. Some apes can learn languages.

Not all languages are spoken ones. Some languages use symbols instead of words. A symbol is something that stands for or reminds us of something else. For example, a heart is often thought of as a symbol for Valentine's Day.

One language that uses symbols instead of words is American Sign Language, or Ameslan for short. This sign language is used by many deaf people. Ameslan is a language that uses sight, not sound. It has a hand sign, or symbol, for each word.

Although they can't form words with their mouths, chimpanzees are good at using their hands. So Washoe was taught Ameslan. She "talks" with her hands in a way any person who knows Ameslan can understand.

Scientists have found that large apes—
chimpanzees and gorillas—are more intelligent
than most other animals. Apes can learn to
communicate in human ways with their trainers.
Some have learned Ameslan. Others have learned
to use words by pushing buttons on a computer.
Still others use pieces of plastic that stand for
words. Wild apes don't use words. They have other
ways of making their feelings known. But apes
have been taught to "talk" with each other.

Surprising things happen as apes learn human
language. Some apes make up new names for
things they have never seen before. Others say
they are sorry when they do something wrong.
Still others tell jokes to their trainers. Teaching
apes to talk has opened a new chapter in our
understanding of the minds of animals.

2

Washoe

Washoe began to learn sign language in 1966. She was born in Africa. While she was still a baby, she was taken to the University of Nevada. There she was raised by Dr. Beatrice Gardner and Dr. Allen Gardner, and later by Dr. Roger Fouts. They wanted to compare her growth with a child's growth. So they didn't put her in a cage. She grew up in a trailer that had rooms like a house. She was given plenty of things to look at and play with.

Scientists had raised chimpanzees as if they were human children before. They had never tried to teach them sign language before, though.

Some university students helped the Gardners train Washoe. There were always people around her to keep her company. The Gardners and their helpers didn't know Ameslan before they got Washoe. They had to learn Ameslan and teach it at the same time. They never spoke aloud to Washoe. They wanted her to learn to understand signs, not spoken words. While they were with her, they didn't speak aloud, even to each other. This helped them learn Ameslan, too. Later deaf people who knew Ameslan well had conversations with Washoe. They could understand most of what she said.

During the first seven months of her training, Washoe learned only four signs. They were gimme, more, up, and sweet. As she got older, Washoe began to learn more quickly. Her trainers repeated signs that matched her activities over and over every day. Some of the first words they taught her were eat, drink, bed, bath, hide, and sweet. Soon Washoe learned to copy her trainers.

Washoe made her first sentence on her own. It was Gimme tickle. Tickling was Washoe's favorite game. So she put two signs together to ask for something she liked a lot.

When she was ready to learn harder "sentences," her trainers taught her words such as you and me and their own names. She learned to ask questions such as You gimme sweet please? and Roger hug Washoe? Washoe didn't just learn a series of signs. She put each word in the right order herself. She could also answer questions as well as ask them.

At first Washoe seemed to think that everyone used sign language. She even tried to use sign language with dogs and cats! Later Washoe could tell when someone didn't know Ameslan. She would make her signs very slowly with new students who came to work with her. She didn't want them to get mixed up.

Washoe liked to look at picture books. At first, though, she thought the pictures were real. She tried to pick the flowers off the page!

After Washoe had learned many words, her trainers used her liking of pictures to test her. They wanted to see how many things in pictures she could name.

Washoe didn't know the signs for all the different things in the pictures. But she was able to put things into groups. For instance, she used the sign car when shown trucks and station wagons. If she did make a mistake, it would be in mixing up things that were alike. She might mix up the signs for two animals, such as cow and dog. But she wouldn't name something very different, such as a kind of food, when shown an animal.

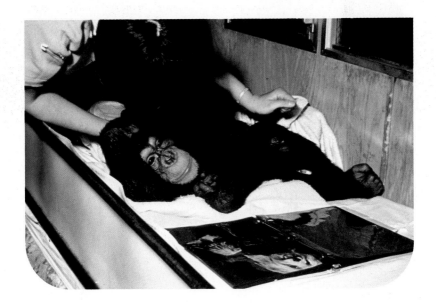

If Washoe didn't know the word for something, she could put together words she did know to describe it. For instance, one day she was taken to a pond where there were some ducks. Washoe named them <u>water birds</u>!

She also used her imagination in other ways. When she was taught the word <u>monkey</u>, she quickly learned to use it for different kinds of monkeys. But there was one monkey she didn't get along with. She called that one a <u>dirty monkey</u>! In fact sometimes she got angry with her trainer and called him <u>Dirty Roger</u>.

3

Sarah

In the late 1960s Washoe was asking for sweets
and tickles in sign language. At the same time
another chimpanzee was learning a different
language in Santa Barbara, California. Dr. David
Premack of the University of California was
teaching a six-year-old chimp named Sarah how to
"read" and "write." Sarah learned to use colored
pieces of plastic as symbols for words. With these
symbols she would make sentences.

Sarah didn't live in human surroundings like Washoe. She stayed in a cage, except during her language lessons. Five days a week, for one hour each day, Sarah met with her trainers. Like the scientists who worked with Washoe, Dr. Premack had students help train Sarah. The students were named Mary and Randy. Unlike Washoe, though, the words Sarah learned were only for "school." She didn't use them all the time to describe what she did and felt.

The backs of the symbols that Sarah worked with had strips of metal on them. The pieces could then be placed on a magnetic board. The board was like a chalkboard in a classroom. Sarah chose to place the symbols under each other on the board. So Sarah's sentences read like those of the Chinese, from top to bottom.

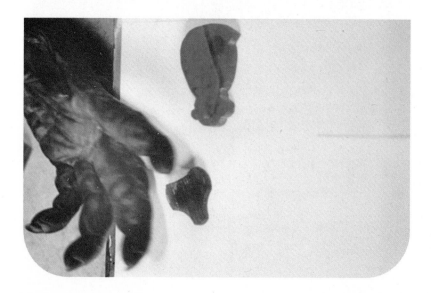

Sarah first learned the names of things she liked, such as fruit. Her trainer would put a slice of fruit on the table. Sarah got to eat this piece of fruit. Then the trainer placed the symbol for the fruit on the table. For instance, the symbol for banana was a pink plastic square. The trainer then put another slice of fruit out of Sarah's reach. Sarah would get the fruit. But first she had to put the symbol of the fruit on the magnetic board. In this way Sarah learned to "read" and "write."

In her lessons Sarah learned not only symbols for words but the right order to put them in. The first sentence she learned was <u>Mary give banana Sarah</u>. Her first sentence was about giving because giving is a natural thing for chimpanzees to do. Wild chimps often give things to each other. Sarah's trainers soon began to show her harder sentences, though. They wanted to see how much Sarah could understand.

Much of Sarah's training depended on comparing things. She learned symbols for <u>same</u> and <u>different</u>. Then she could answer questions such as <u>apple same as orange?</u> Sarah became very good at answering this kind of question. She then began to learn symbols for colors, sizes, shapes, and amounts.

The trainers tested Sarah's understanding of amounts such as <u>all</u>, <u>many</u>, <u>one</u>, and <u>several</u> by having her read instructions. The instructions told different amounts of candy or crackers to put in a dish. If she followed them correctly, she was allowed to eat what was in the dish.

Sarah figured out how to follow the test instructions and still choose her own reward. When she "read" <u>Sarah insert none cracker dish</u>, she did what she was told to do. She didn't put any crackers in the dish. She put a piece of candy in the dish instead! Then she ate it. The next time that she was told to put in crackers Sarah put all the candy in the dish and ran away with her prize!

Scientists learned a lot from what Sarah learned. They found that apes can connect the idea of a thing with a symbol. For example, Sarah's trainers asked her to describe the symbol for <u>apple</u>. This symbol was a small blue triangle. But Sarah called it large, red, and round. It was once thought that only humans could think of things in this way.

When Sarah was fully grown, trainers couldn't work with her any more. An adult chimpanzee is three to five times as strong as a person. When chimpanzees don't do well in their lessons, they often get angry. They can have temper tantrums. So it was safest for younger chimpanzees to take Sarah's place in "school."

4
Lana

Some chimpanzees use sign language. Others can "read" and "write" with plastic symbols. A chimpanzee named Lana, however, has another way to "write." She knows a language called Yerkish. It was made up for her to use with a computer. Lana talks with people by pushing buttons on a computer keyboard.

Yerkish was invented at the Yerkes Primate Center in Atlanta, Georgia. Dr. Duane Rumbaugh, a scientist at the center, first thought of the computer language. Now he and Dr. Timothy Gill train Lana to "speak" Yerkish.

Lana's keyboard has room for 125 buttons. Each key, or button, has a symbol on it that stands for a word. The words in Yerkish look like designs. For instance, please looks like an arrow. The symbol for <u>machine</u> looks like a triangle with a line above it.

When Lana presses a key, the symbol flashes on a screen above her. She can see the sentence that she is making. Her trainer sits at another keyboard in a room next to hers. He, too, sees what Lana is saying as she pushes keys. Lana's trainers often answer her or ask her more questions. When the trainer tells her something in Yerkish, that sentence shows on the screen, too. It is like a written conversation.

Lana's trainers want to make sure that Lana understands the symbols she is using. So every day the symbols on the keyboard are moved to different keys. Otherwise Lana might know a word just by where it is on the keyboard.

Lana lives in the room with the computer keyboard all the time. She can talk to the computer 24 hours a day. Lana uses the keys to ask for anything she wants—such as food, drink, or music. As long as she pushes the keys in the right order, Lana gets what she wants.

Lana makes real sentences with the symbols on the keyboard. All her sentences must end with periods. Her questions must begin with question marks. If Lana wants something from the machine, she must begin her sentence with <u>please</u>. Lana's trainers haven't taught her in this way so that she will be polite. Rather, these are ways of telling things to the machine. For instance, the word <u>please</u> warns the machine that Lana is going to ask for something.

Sometimes Lana makes mistakes in sentences. Maybe the words are in the wrong order. Maybe she used the wrong word to say something—such as <u>eat milk</u> instead of <u>drink milk</u>. If there is a mistake, the machine either makes a noise or turns off the light on the sentence. Lana "erases" her mistakes by pushing the key for <u>period</u>. That tells the computer her sentence is done. Then she can begin again.

All Lana's food is given to her by the computer. She can ask for different kinds of food. Often she tells the computer, <u>Please machine give piece of apple period.</u>

Food isn't the only thing Lana asks the computer to give her. She can also ask to look out the window. Sometimes she asks the computer to show a movie or a slide show. Sometimes she asks to hear some music. Her favorite music is rock, and she likes movies about chimpanzees.

Like Washoe, Lana invents names for things she doesn't know the words for. Once Tim came to visit Lana with an orange in his hand. Lana wanted the orange. But there was no symbol on her keyboard for that fruit. How could she get it? She knew her colors and the symbol for <u>apple</u>. So she wrote, <u>?Tim give apple which is orange color.</u>

Lana's life isn't as lonely as it may sound. When her trainers are around, they come into her room to play with her. Lana has learned to begin conversations with people. One thing she often writes is <u>Please Tim come into room</u>. Then Tim and Lana often play one of Lana's favorite games. As Tim enters, Lana asks him on her keyboard, <u>?Tim tickle Lana</u>. Tim starts to move his fingers to the <u>no</u> key. Lana pulls at his fingers until they press <u>yes</u>. With that Lana leaps across the room with Tim right behind her. He catches Lana and tickles her as she hoots with joy.

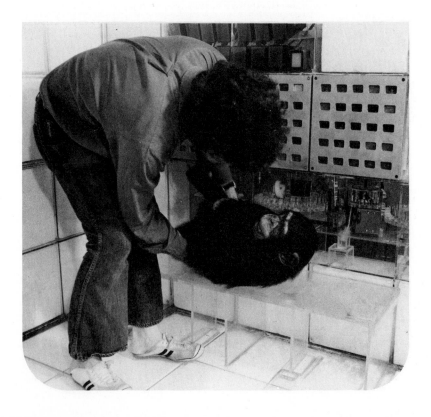

5

Koko

Almost all apes that have been taught to use words are chimpanzees. There is one gorilla who can use language, though. Her name is Koko. According to her trainer, Koko knows almost 400 words.

Koko lives in a trailer at Stanford University in California. Penny Patterson is her trainer. To most people, gorillas are rather frightening. In the wild, though, they are really shy, gentle animals. If they are either mistreated or frightened, gorillas can indeed be dangerous. Young gorillas that have been raised like children can be friends to human beings, however. Penny has shown that through her work with Koko. She thinks of this half-grown gorilla more as a friend than as a pet.

Koko can understand spoken language, although she uses Ameslan to "talk" with people. Besides naming objects and asking for things she likes, Koko can answer questions about how she feels. She knows how to use signs for <u>hungry</u>, <u>fine</u>, <u>sad</u>, <u>happy</u>, and <u>afraid</u>.

Once a reporter asked Koko whom she liked better—Penny or the assistant trainer, Ann Southcombe. Koko didn't want to tell the reporter! She liked both Penny and Ann. After a long wait she gave the sign for <u>bad question</u>.

Another time Koko did something she wasn't supposed to do. She tore up a sponge. Shaking it, Penny asked, "What is this?" At first Koko didn't answer. At last she signed, <u>trouble</u>. Then she reached out to hug Penny, hoping to be forgiven.

Like Washoe, Koko puts learned words together to make names for new objects. Her names make sense, too. When she first saw a ring, she called it <u>finger bracelet</u>. Her name for a zebra was <u>white tiger</u>.

Koko likes to "talk," and she uses her language a lot. She talks to herself when she is playing with dolls. She talks to the dolls, too. Once she tried to talk on the telephone. A shocked telephone operator traced the call back to Koko's trailer. The operator had thought the call was from a dying man.

Penny is worried about what may happen to Koko if she ever has to live in a zoo with other gorillas. She knows Koko wouldn't be happy there. Penny wouldn't want to be apart from Koko, either.

6

A Lot Left to Learn

The apes who have learned sign languages or symbol languages have surprised their trainers. These animals have shown more ability to think than many people believed animals could have. So far no one really knows how much apes can learn. For one thing trainers have worked only with young apes. Could an adult chimpanzee or gorilla use language even better? That is something scientists would like to find out.

Scientists would also like to know if apes could teach language to other apes. Chimpanzees who know words do use them with each other. Could they teach words to an ape who knew no words, though? Washoe, the first ape to use words, had a baby. Scientists wanted to see if she would teach sign language to her baby. But the baby died. Penny Patterson hopes that Koko will be a mother some day. Penny thinks that Koko will teach Ameslan to her baby.

Scientists wonder what would happen if an ape that knew a language were set free in the jungle. Would the ape pass the language on to wild apes? Would the ape make up new signs for things it found in the wild? Scientists don't know the answers to these questions yet. No "talking" chimpanzee has yet been returned to the wild.

Perhaps the biggest question that many scientists have is what apes—and other animals—think about. In teaching language to apes, scientists have opened the doors of animals' minds to humans. Scientists are learning what these animals can and can't do. An ape might be able to learn a language so well that all its thoughts would be in the language. Who knows what we then might find out about the minds of animals?

The Blizzard

Michael could tell that the storm was going to be a bad one. He didn't know that it would put him in danger—or that it would give him a chance to prove something important to his father.

1

Storm on the Way

Michael Redfern threw his body against the gate. He pushed with all his might. "I don't think I can do it!" he shouted. "The wind is too strong." The icy wind almost drowned out his words.

"Push harder, then!" Michael's father shouted back. Mr. Redfern was on the other side of the covered corral. He was trying to mend a tear in the wire. His jacket and old hat were covered with snow. Michael couldn't see his father's face, but he could hear the tone of his voice. It sounded angry.

Mr. Redfern had looked and sounded angry for the past year. Michael thought that it had all begun when Michael's brother George had died. Today Mr. Redfern's mood was worse than usual. Maybe it was just the storm. The temperature had started to drop in the morning. Since then Michael and his father had been hard at work. The snow was already falling heavily, and a real blizzard was on the way. The weather reporter on the radio said so. Mr. Redfern didn't need a weather reporter to tell him that. He had been sheep ranching in these Montana hills all his life. He knew all the signs of an oncoming blizzard.

Michael knew the signs, too—the gray clouds, the icy cold, the wind whipping in from the north. He also knew that for a sheep rancher this was the worst time of year for a blizzard. The winter was almost over. It was the end of March. Many of the ewes were due to lamb. If the lambs were born on the range in a heavy storm, they would have no chance of living. That was why Michael and his father had been struggling all day to bring the ewes into the corral. That was why he had to get the gate closed.

Michael took a deep breath. Making a great effort, he gave another push. He could feel his father looking at him. He pushed as hard as he could. The wind seemed to be blowing harder than ever. He dug his heels into the frozen ground. Slowly the gate moved. He pushed harder and it moved forward again. At last he heard the lock click shut.

The sheep moved around inside the locked corral. They were bleating into the howling wind. Michael looked up to see if his father would say anything. His father just turned away and headed for the house.

He could have said something, Michael thought. He lowered his head into the wind and followed. It hadn't been easy bringing in the sheep and closing the heavy gate. Michael caught up with his father as he opened the back door. Mr. Redfern looked old and tired. His skin was creased from years of facing into cold winter winds and hot summer suns.

"Well, we did it, Dad," Michael said hopefully. "No blizzard is going to beat us." He stepped into the house after his father. He stamped the snow off his boots and rubbed his hands together to warm them. "That gate just gave me a little trouble."

Mr. Redfern took off his jacket and hat. He hung them on a peg by the door. "George could have done it easily," was all he said.

2
An Accident

Michael had worked so hard to get the gate closed. It seemed as if his father didn't care at all. Michael almost couldn't believe what his father had just said. George again! Why did his father always compare him with George? He was tired of hearing about George.

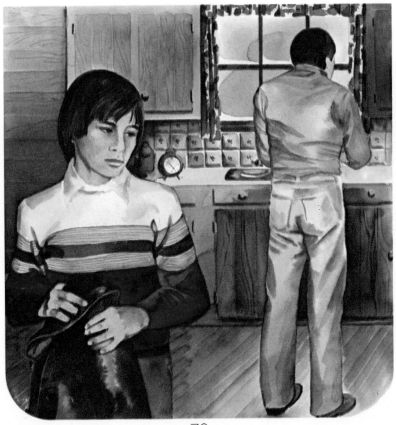

George was Michael's older brother. He had died a year ago, and his death had hit Mr. Redfern hard. His older boy had been everything he wanted in a son. George had been strong and tall. He had been a star player on the football team at school. Michael always felt that he couldn't live up to what his brother had been.

"Better wash up," Mr. Redfern said now. He headed for the stairs that led to the second floor of the house. "And put on a pot of hot chocolate. I can feel this cold right to the center of my bones."

"Sure, Dad," Michael answered, trying to sound cheerful. He didn't want his father to know how much he hurt inside.

Michael started to make the hot chocolate. Then he began washing the dishes left in the sink from lunch. Michael's mother had died when he was eight. Now, with George gone, there was just his father and himself. They had to do all the work inside and outside the house.

There was plenty of work, too—cooking and cleaning and making repairs. They still hadn't gotten around to painting the kitchen. Michael also remembered another important chore. The boards on the stairs needed to be replaced. That third step was in very bad shape. Michael sighed. His cold hands tingled as he dipped them into the hot dishwater.

Michael thought back to closing the gate of the sheep pen. He wished he were stronger. If only he could gain some weight. Then he might make the football team like George, but it looked hopeless. Michael was thin and light. No amount of food seemed to fill him out.

He heard his father moving about upstairs. Then his heavy footsteps started down the shaky flight of stairs. I had better fix those boards tomorrow, Michael thought. Some day someone is going to forget to skip that third step.

"Oh!" The sudden shout broke into Michael's thoughts. He heard the sound of splintering wood. He spun around, dropping the cup he was about to wash.

"Dad!" He rushed forward, but he was too late to break his father's fall. Mr. Redfern had stepped through the rotten wood on the third step. He had lost his balance and tumbled to the floor below. He lay at the foot of the stairs. His left leg was bent beneath him at a strange angle.

"Dad, are you all right?" Michael asked, leaning down to help him.

"Of course, I'm all . . ." Mr. Redfern began. But when he tried to get up, he let out a sudden cry of pain. He dropped back. "Michael!" he cried. "Something is wrong!"

3

A Bad Break

Michael dropped to his knees. He stared in horror at his father's twisted leg. He could see his father was in great pain. Beads of sweat had suddenly appeared on his forehead.

Michael felt a wave of fear come over him. He was used to his father being strong and able.

"It's my leg," Mr. Redfern groaned. "It's twisted or something."

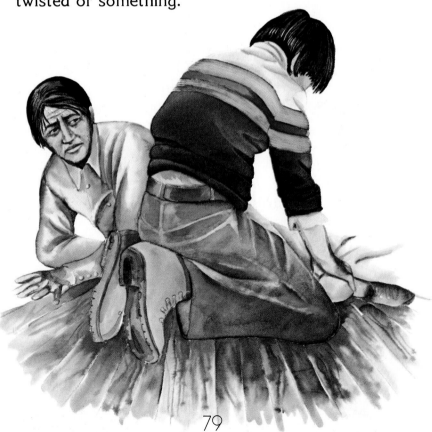

"Let me see." Michael reached out to feel his father's left leg. At the first touch Mr. Redfern cried out in pain.

"It's more than twisted, Dad," Michael said. "I think it's broken." Michael quickly got a pair of scissors from the chest at the foot of the stairs. "I'm going to cut your pant leg so I can see better," he said. "I'll try to be careful."

Mr. Redfern nodded and braced himself. He didn't say a word as his son cut the cloth and folded it back. It was worse than Michael had thought. He had taken a first aid course at school. He was sure that his father's leg was broken. He shook at the sight of a great lump halfway down the calf. It was the leg bone, almost, but not quite, poking through the skin. His father needed medical help—soon.

"It's pretty bad, Dad," Michael said, standing up. "I'm sure that your leg is broken. We've got to get you straight to the hospital. The sooner we get you there the better."

"I don't need any hospital," Mr. Redfern said. "I'll be all right if I just rest for a while."

Michael had already raced to the phone and was dialing the operator. He heard one ring and then another. Finally he heard the operator's voice.

"I want the Danville County Hospital," Michael said. "It's an emergency. My father is . . ."

Before Michael could say another word, he heard a click on the other end of the line. Then there was silence. The phone was dead. Michael tried dialing again, but it was no use. The storm must have blown down the lines.

He hung up the phone and looked at his father. There was only one thing for Michael to do.

"Dad," he said, "I'm going to take you to the hospital."

"You?" said Mr. Redfern. His face was white from the pain. "But there is a blizzard blowing out there. Remember, you just got your learner's permit last month. You've never taken the car out in this kind of weather."

"Don't worry, I can do it," Michael answered. His heart was pounding in his chest, but he tried to keep calm. He reminded himself that he was the best student in his driver education class. He had seen worse winters and bigger blizzards than this. He could do it. After all he didn't have to be a football player like George to drive a car.

4

Into the Blizzard

Mr. Redfern didn't protest when Michael helped him into the back seat of the car. Michael covered him with blankets. He put a sheepskin rug under the broken leg to help keep it still. The pain was so great that Mr. Redfern could barely keep from passing out. He shut his eyes and lay still beneath the blankets. Michael was on his own. There was nothing his father could do to help him.

Michael was shaking. He wasn't sure whether it was from the cold or from fear. He slid in behind the steering wheel. Then he started the engine. There was plenty of gas. The oil had been checked the day before yesterday. Antifreeze had been poured into the radiator at the start of the winter. The antifreeze kept the water in the radiator from freezing. When you lived in this kind of country, you had to remember things like that. You had to think ahead.

Michael thought ahead now as he backed the car carefully out of the garage. The hospital was 50 km away in Danville. If he took the shortcut over Wolf Mountain, he would cut the distance in half. He wondered whether he could make it in this weather.

The windshield wipers brushed the falling snow from side to side on the window. The car traveled over the bumpy driveway and turned onto the main road. Mr. Redfern let out a low moan with each bump they passed over.

Michael's hands felt like ice on the steering wheel. The turn-off for Wolf Mountain Road was just ahead. He had to decide whether to take the turn-off. Just then he saw a sign that made him come to a halt. <u>Chains Required</u>. He had been so worried about his father that he had forgotten. Chains were always required on that road in winter weather. Now he had to stop and get the chains out of the trunk. It would take time to fit them over the rear wheels. He could feel the minutes ticking away. But it would be foolish to go on without chains.

"Michael," his father groaned as Michael got back into the car.

"It's okay, Dad," Michael said. He tried to sound sure of himself. "We're going to make it."

More than ever, Michael felt pressed for time. He no longer wondered whether he should take the short cut. Now he would have to try Wolf Mountain Road. He turned off the main road and shifted into low gear. The car began to climb the steep road. He could feel the crunch of the chains against the snow. The wind howled through the trees. What would happen if a tree fell right across the road?

Michael shivered and tried not to think about it. He had to keep his mind on his driving. The car climbed to the crest and then started down. Michael peered out through the windshield at the electric wires, strung on poles along the road. The wires were swaying in the strong wind. They crossed from one side to the other a short distance ahead.

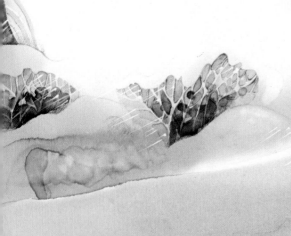

All at once, a shower of sparks shot up from one of the poles. The heavy electric cable shook and swayed. Then it dropped to the ground. Michael slowly put on the brakes and stopped the car. He stared in horror at the cable. It was lying like a great black snake across Wolf Mountain Road. It was a live wire! He didn't dare drive across it.

5

The Light in the Snow

Michael knew he couldn't drive over the live wire. But it was too late to turn back. He had gone 13 km already. Danville was only 12 km away. He looked at his father lying on the back seat with his eyes closed. Mr. Redfern was breathing hard, barely aware of what was going on.

If only he hadn't taken the Wolf Mountain Road. In a strange way Michael was thankful that his father wasn't aware of what was happening. At least he couldn't say that George would have known better. Michael stared hopefully at the snow.

All at once he remembered something. The Thompsons lived on Wolf Mountain. Though their phone was most likely out, they had a CB radio. A CB radio would work even in this blizzard. Mr. or Mrs. Thompson could call the highway patrol on the emergency channel. The highway patrol could call the hospital. An ambulance could be sent out to bring Mr. Redfern to the hospital. Michael wasn't sure that he could find the Thompsons' house in the storm, but he had to try. "Dad," he said, "I'm going to try to get help."

Mr. Redfern nodded slightly, so Michael knew that he had heard. His eyes were still closed. Michael made sure that his father was well covered with blankets. "I'll be back soon. I'll have a doctor with me," he said. "You'll be all right, Dad. I promise."

The whole world outside the car was white. It was hard to tell where the road was. Michael kept his eyes on the telephone poles. He knew the telephone poles went straight along the side of the road. He knew the Thompsons' house was just past the spot where the cable had fallen. He figured that if he walked straight down the road he would reach the house.

Michael's feet felt like ice. The wind blew so
hard that it almost knocked him over. Still he
didn't stop. You can do it, he told himself. You can
do it. Just as he was beginning to question his
own words, he saw a light shining through the
snow. It was the Thompsons' house. Nothing had
ever looked so good to Michael before. He
struggled the last few steps through the snowdrifts.
Then he pounded on the door.

Mrs. Thompson opened it. In what seemed like no time she had called the highway patrol. Michael wanted to go straight back to the car and wait with his father. Mrs. Thompson made him stay until the ambulance came. "Your father will be all right if he's covered up well," Mrs. Thompson told him. "You'll have frostbitten feet if you go out in that storm again. The temperature is most likely well below zero now."

Finally the ambulance driver and her helper stopped at the Thompsons' house to pick up Michael. By the time they arrived Michael was sick with worry. Suppose his father had tried to move? Suppose the blankets weren't warm enough?

The ambulance went to where the live wire lay across the road. The paramedics and Michael walked quickly to Mr. Redfern's car. A quick check by the paramedics showed that Mr. Redfern was all right.

"You did well to bring him in, Michael," the ambulance driver said. "That is one of the worst breaks I've seen in a long time."

"Michael," Mr. Redfern said faintly as he was moved onto a stretcher. His eyes were filled with pain. He reached out and took his son's hand. "Thank you," he whispered.

Michael didn't know what to say or do. He didn't remember his father ever thanking him for anything before.

"I'm lucky to have a son like you," Mr. Redfern went on. Michael looked into his father's eyes. Suddenly Michael felt as if he were going to laugh and cry at the same time. Mr. Redfern gripped his son's hand more tightly. "I'm proud of you, Michael," he whispered. "Very proud."

Creatures
of the
Deep

The ocean is full of strange creatures. We know about some of them. But others, such as sea serpents and giant squids, may always be mysteries.

1

Imaginary Creatures

The sea is full of mysteries. It isn't simply like another country. It's more like another world. We can't live in this sea world. We can't even see into it very far. Scientists and divers have explored only a tiny part of it. Beneath its surface lie great mountains and valleys. In some places the sea is deeper than the highest mountain is high. We can only guess what creatures might live in such a setting.

Stories about sea monsters have been told for thousands of years. Some of the creatures these stories tell about are mermaids, giant octopuses, and sea serpents. People have been surprised to find that some of these monsters are real animals. Other sea creatures have turned out to be only stories.

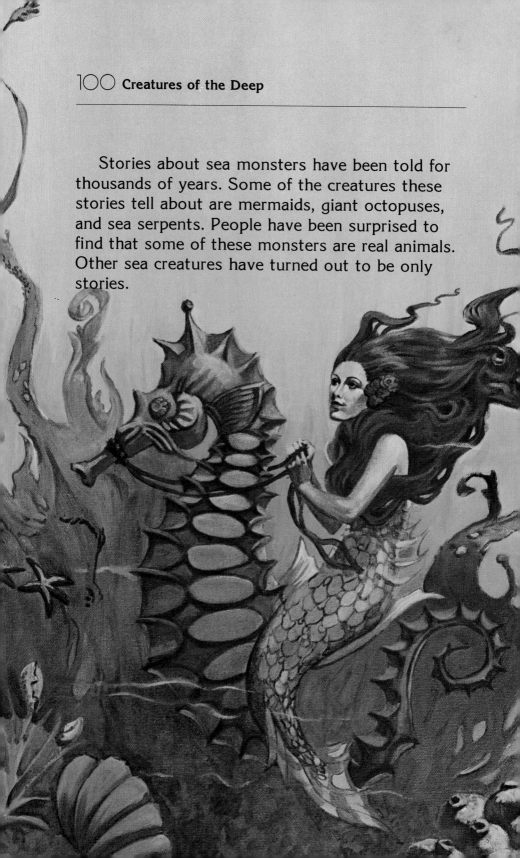

Long ago many people thought that the world underneath the sea must be much like our own. They thought that for every land animal there was a sea animal to match. They knew that there were sea horses and sea lions. They said that there must be sea tigers, sea pigs, and sea elephants as well. And sea people? Well, they thought, of course there were sea people.

Many people believed in mermaids in those days. According to the old stories, a mermaid looked like a beautiful woman. She had long green or golden hair. From the waist down she had the tail of a fish. It was said that mermaids liked to sit and sing on the rocks that jutted out from the sea. Their sweet music would draw sailors closer and closer. Finally the sailors' ships would crash onto the rocks. It was said that if mermaids got angry their singing would cause storms to arise. Mermaids were also thought to have the power to tell the future.

People also believed in mermen—half fish, half man. A Greek story more than 2,000 years old tells of a man named Glaucus. He was a fisherman who loved the sea. One day Glaucus was watching a fish he had just caught. The fish was eating a plant that grew on the shore. As Glaucus watched, the fish became strong again. It flopped back into the sea. Interested, Glaucus ate a little of the plant. Suddenly he felt that he too must throw himself into the waves. As he sank, his legs grew together into a fish's tail. His hair flowed long and green like seaweed. It was lucky that Glaucus loved the sea, for he had become a merman.

Other stories tell of mermaids marrying humans. One story is about mermaids who take on the shapes of seals. On moonlit nights they swim to shore. There they leave their sealskins on the sand. The mermaids no longer have fish tails, but look like beautiful women. They dance together on the sand. Sometimes a man is watching the mermaids as they dance. He hides one of the sealskins. Then the mermaid it belongs to is trapped on shore. She must either tell his future or marry him. If the mermaid marries him, she still might find her sealskin again, even years later. She would then put it on at once and swim off into the sea.

Several hundred years ago some people thought they had found real mermaids. These mermaids were reported by the first explorers who returned from America. These mermaids were not at all beautiful. What the explorers really had seen were manatees, or sea cows. These odd, harmless animals can still be seen in Florida. They are long and very fat. Their fat silly-looking faces are mud gray in color. They stare at people in a very human way.

Today few people believe in mermaids. But we can guess how the stories first came about. Seals have beautiful dark eyes, with an almost human look in them. Some people might have believed that seals were sea people in disguise. So stories were told of seals who took off their skins and became women.

Mermaids and mermen seem to have lived only in people's minds. Many people wonder if stories about other sea creatures are true or false. As time goes on, we are learning more and more about the sea. Some day we may know if these stories are about real animals.

2

The Sea Serpent

It's one thing to tell stories about a sea monster. It's another thing to see one. Captain Peter M'Quhae of the British ship <u>Daedalus</u> prided himself on being a wise person. No wise person, he thought, would believe tales of sea monsters. In 1848 something changed his mind. His ship was sailing on the South Atlantic Ocean on an August afternoon. Captain M'Quhae was walking with two of his officers on the deck. Suddenly a sailor came running up.

"Sir!" he said. "Something is coming toward the ship!" He pointed out at the water.

Captain M'Quhae looked. He saw what seemed to be a snake swimming, holding its head above the water. But what he could see of the animal was 20 m long! Its neck just behind the head was as thick as a tree trunk. Now it was passing the ship at about 25 km an hour. The four men watched until the serpent was gone.

When he reached land, Captain M'Quhae reported what he had seen. His account was in all the newspapers. Most scientists refused to believe him. Other people had made up stories of sea serpents. So scientists thought Captain M'Quhae was making up his story, too. They made fun of Captain M'Quhae in the newspapers. Soon M'Quhae wished he had never said anything at all.

Yet Captain M'Quhae wasn't the only person to see a sea serpent. In 1817 a sea serpent spent several weeks off the Massachusetts coast. It was seen by hundreds of people. One man had been very close to it.

Other ships' captains, too, said that they had seen sea serpents. Captain George Hope of the British ship Fly had seen a sea serpent years before Captain M'Quhae had. Captain Hope had been afraid to print his story, though. Then he read M'Quhae's account. He felt that he, too, should tell what he had seen. Captain Hope was the first person to get a view of the whole animal, from head to tail. The sea in the Gulf of California was calm and clear that day. Captain Hope could see the animal swimming along the sea bottom. It was shaped like an alligator, but its neck was much longer. Instead of legs it had four large flippers.

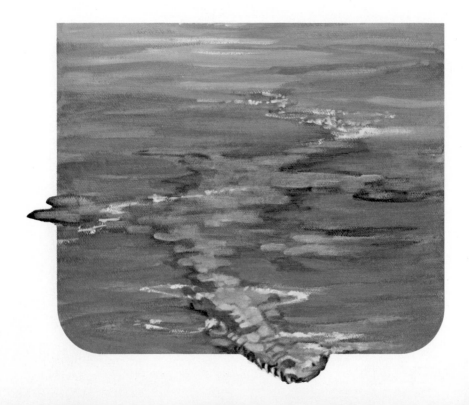

During World War I, Captain F. W. Dean of the British ship <u>Hilary</u> was called to the bridge. His ship was passing through the North Sea. The officer on watch had seen a strange animal lying in the water. Only its snakelike head and neck were showing. The neck alone was at least 7 m long. Captain Dean ordered his crew to fire at the animal. The crew fired ten rounds without hitting the serpent. It lay quietly watching them. The next shot was very close. Then came a clean hit. Water spouted up, splashing in every direction. When the splashing stopped, the animal was gone.

People tried to explain the sea serpent in many ways. They said that a row of leaping dolphins could look like a great snake. But even 50 dolphins couldn't look like a head and neck lifted out of the water. Some people said that a lump of seaweed could look like a sea serpent. But seaweed does not swim at 25 km an hour. Other people said that it must have been a big eel or a whale. But seamen such as Captain Dean and Captain M'Quhae knew what seaweed and dolphins looked like. They had seen many eels and whales. What they saw was something different. It was something we still can't explain.

3

The Monster of Loch Ness

During the 1800s many people said they had seen sea serpents. Strangely enough all the accounts of sea serpents seem to fit the same picture. They all tell of an animal shaped like an alligator, but with a longer neck. The animal had flippers instead of legs. Some people, such as Captain M'Quhae, saw only the head, neck, and back of the animal. Others told of seeing flippers when the animal lifted itself above the water. But all the accounts say that the animal was dark brown or black in color. Most agree that it was about 20 or 30 m long. None of the accounts says that the animal attacked the ship or tried to kill the sailors. This sea monster seems as quiet and shy as most wild animals.

These stories of sea serpents fit another animal as well. Unlike the sea serpents, though, this animal has been sighted in a lake. Loch Ness is a lake in Scotland. (<u>Loch</u> means "lake.") It is the largest inland body of water in Great Britain. Mist and fog blow over its dark, rippling surface. Many people believe that some strange monster lives in its deep waters.

Some scientists now believe that the sea serpent and the so-called Loch Ness monster may be the same kind of animal. Like the sea serpent, the Loch Ness monster is also pictured as dark in color. It is said to have a snakelike neck and head. The accounts report that it is between 7 and 20 m long.

One night in 1933 two people driving home along the shore heard loud splashing in the loch. A long, dark, humped body burst suddenly from the water. It shot through the waves. Then it dove down again in a swirl of foam. Soon other people were reporting that they had seen the monster. During the last 40 years it has supposedly been seen dozens of times. Often sightings are reported at the same time by people on different sides of the loch.

Some people are now trying to prove the existence of "Nessie," as the monster is called. They are taking pictures under water and using sonar. Sonar has shown that there are large moving things in the loch. The water of Loch Ness is so muddy that no camera can shoot anything very far away. One picture taken in 1975 may show the monster. In the picture there seems to be a small head, a long neck, and two large flippers. It may be that the proof for Nessie isn't far away.

4

Giant Squids and Octopuses

For thousands of years people have told stories of giant octopuses and squids. There are tales of octopuses so big that sailors thought they were islands. The sailors landed on the octopuses to cook their food. Other stories tell of octopuses attacking large sailing ships. Old pictures show the octopus winding its hungry tentacles around the masts of ships. In other pictures the octopus is grabbing a sailor from the deck.

Could there be such monsters? "Of course not," said many scientists. Until the year 1861 people thought that giant squids and octopuses were just stories.

In 1861 the French ship <u>Alecton</u> was sailing peacefully on the Atlantic Ocean. Suddenly the ship's lookout spotted something drifting on the waves. It was a giant squid. Its bright red body was about 6 m long. Its tentacles were at least as long as its body. Each eye was nearly 50 cm across.

The sailors did their best to catch the monster. They threw harpoons and fired their cannon at it. The cannon balls didn't seem to hurt it. The harpoons wouldn't hold in its soft flesh. At last one man threw a rope around the fins near the squid's tail end. The sailors tried to pull the monster aboard. Again the flesh was so soft that the rope cut through it. The squid sank out of sight, leaving its fins behind. The sailors saved the fins for proof of their story. Long before they got home the fins decayed and had to be thrown out.

The whole crew swore to the story of the giant squid, but it was no use. "Too much sun," said many scientists with a smile. Many people didn't know what to believe. Who was right—the sailors who said they saw the squid? Or the scientists who thought it was impossible for such an animal to exist?

In 1873 this question came up once again in people's minds. This time no one could say the monster was just another story. It began when a small fishing boat was moving slowly along the coast of Newfoundland.

"Look!" shouted one of the fishers. "What is that?"

His two friends shook their heads. They had no idea what the thing could be. It was a great, dark, shapeless mass floating on the water not far away. It was going up and down with the waves.

"Let's take a closer look. Whatever it is, we can keep it as salvage and find some use for it."

They rowed over to the floating shape. One of them stuck his boat hook into it to pull it nearer. Suddenly the thing rose up. It swelled higher and higher like a great black umbrella. Two green eyes stared out of the blackness. Two huge tentacles grabbed the small boat.

The men leaped back. "Quick!" cried one. "The hatchet!" The boat rocked wildly as the hatchet rose and fell on the tentacles. Black clouds of fluid spurted from the monster. Then, suddenly, it disappeared into the dark waters. The two tentacles still twitched like live things in the bottom of the boat.

The fishers cut up one of the tentacles for bait. The other tentacle was measured by the man who reported the story. Two meters of the tentacle had already gone into the bait box. What was left of it was more than three times as long.

For several years, giant octopuses were seen often along the Newfoundland coast. Perhaps an earthquake under the sea had forced them to leave their caves. There was no longer any question of whether these sea monsters existed. The chopped-off tentacles were proof enough. Later several giant octopuses were caught alive.

We still don't know much about these animals. We can't even guess how big a giant octopus or squid might grow. Whales have been found with the marks from huge tentacles on their sides. The owners of these tentacles must be far bigger than any animal we have yet seen.

5

A Monster from the Past

"Stop! Don't throw it back!"

The fisher lifted his head, surprised. "Why not, captain? It doesn't look like a food fish to me."

"No," the captain agreed. "But did you ever see anything like it before?"

The big fish was thrashing about in the net. It was biting at everything in reach. It must have been nearly 2 m long and weighed more than 40 kg. It had a large, heavy head. These fishers had seen fish all their lives. To them this fish looked strange indeed. For one thing it had two fins on its back, where other fish have one. There was something stiff, almost wooden, in the way it moved. It seemed as if its backbone went all the way down to the end of its tail.

The captain of the fishing boat made up his mind. "We'll take it home with us," he said.

"But captain, we can't keep it alive till we reach East London."

"I know," sighed the captain.

"Captain, when it dies, it will stink up the whole boat."

"It sure will. But it's got to go to a museum."

The fish died, of course. The fishers put it on ice for the rest of the trip. It was smelling pretty bad by the time they got it to East London, South Africa. They brought it to the museum. The museum curator, Miss Latimer, knew that the big, ugly fish was something special. She wrote to Dr. J. L. B. Smith, an expert on fish. She asked him to come at once. Together they could study the strange fish.

Before Dr. Smith could get there, almost all of the fish had decayed. It was falling to pieces. There was no way that Miss Latimer could save the whole fish. So she had it cleaned and skinned. She had the skin mounted and saved the skull. Then she had the rest of the fish quickly taken away.

When Dr. Smith arrived, he was sorry not to have the whole fish to work on. But enough was left for him to see what kind of fish it was. It was a coelacanth.

This coelacanth was found in 1938. Until then scientists thought that coelacanths had been extinct since the age of dinosaurs. (Something that is extinct is no longer existing in living form.) The last dinosaurs were dying out 60 million years ago. The last coelacanth fossils came from that time. (A fossil is the hard remains or traces of a plant or animal of a past age.) Even in the age of dinosaurs the coelacanth had been a "living fossil." That is, it really belonged to an age long before the age of dinosaurs. Its own age, the Devonian Age, ended 275 million years ago. At that time the coelacanth should really have become extinct. Instead it lived on, unchanging, in the deep world of the sea.

Since 1938 many people have looked for coelacanths in the sea's waters. A second coelacanth was found in 1952 off the coast of Africa. This time scientists had a chance to study the fish more closely. They wanted to learn even more about this living fossil.

Many people are surprised to learn that sharks, too, are living fossils. They come from the same age as the coelacanth comes from. Scientists thought that they knew every kind of shark that existed. In 1976 they found out that they were wrong.

A U.S. Navy boat had dropped its sea anchor near Hawaii. A sea anchor looks like a parachute. It keeps boats from rolling about. To a hungry shark it looked like food. Under water the shark attacked the sea anchor. Soon it became trapped in the anchor and died. When the shark was pulled aboard, it turned out to be a new kind of shark. This new shark has a big rounded head with huge jaws. Its body tapers down to a thin tail. Scientists have named it "Megamouth," which means "big mouth." Megamouth is nearly 5 m long and weighs more than 500 kg. Yet until now it had remained a secret of the sea.

We can be sure that the sea hasn't run out of surprises. People talked about giant squids and octopuses as if they were made-up creatures. But living proof of them was found in the 1800s. The Loch Ness monster and sea serpents may be real animals, too. Until 1938 no one even thought that coelacanths were still living. Who knows what we may some day find in the sea's deep waters?

Words from the Stories

alpaca (al pac a; al·'pak·ə) A cloth made from the long, silky wool of the alpaca, an animal of South America that looks like a sheep.

Jack's **alpaca** jacket is both light and warm.

ambulance (am bu lance; 'am·byə·ləns) A special kind of car for carrying sick and wounded people.

The sick man was put in an **ambulance** and taken to the hospital.

Ameslan (Am es lan; 'am·əs·lan) The abbreviation for American Sign Language.

Deaf people use their hands to "speak" **Ameslan.**

antifreeze (an ti freeze; 'an·ti·'frēz) A substance that is added to a liquid, such as water, to keep it from freezing.

As soon as winter began, Denise put **antifreeze** in the car radiator.

CB radio (CB ra di o; CB 'rā·dē·ō) A special kind of radio with a channel that anyone can use to talk with people far away. **CB** is short for citizens band.

Truck drivers use their **CB radios** to tell one another about road conditions.

coelacanth (coe la canth; 'sē·lə·kanth) A large fish that existed over 275 million years ago.

The fishers looked at the **coelacanth** in their net and wondered what it was.

computer (com pu ter; kəm·'pyo͞o·tər) A machine
that can store great amounts of information
and figure out problems very quickly.

Dr. Ito waited a few moments for the **computer**
to answer her question.

corral (cor ral; kə·'ral) An enclosed space or pen
for livestock such as horses, cattle, or sheep.

The rancher and his daughters rounded up the
wild horses and put them in the **corral.**

curator (cu ra tor; kyo͞o·'rā·tər) A person in charge
of a museum or zoo.

The boys took the old bone they had found to
the **curator** of a natural history museum.

decay (de cay; di·'kā) To rot.

After the fish had been dead for a few days, it
started to **decay.**

depot (de pot; 'dep·ō) A place where military
supplies are stored.

Clothing for the troops was kept in the army
depot.

Devonian Age (De vo ni an Age; di·'vō·ni·an āj) A
period in the history of the earth which ended
275 million years ago.

Most of the animals that lived during the
Devonian Age no longer exist.

dinosaurs (di no saurs; 'dī·nə·sôrs) Very large
animals that died off millions of years ago.

Long before humans existed, **dinosaurs** roamed the earth.

emergency (e mer gen cy; i·'mûr·jən·sē) An unexpected happening that calls for quick action.

When she told us it was an **emergency,** we dropped everything and ran to help her.

ewe (ewe; yo͞o) A female sheep.

The **ewe** gave birth to her lamb in early spring.

extinct (ex tinct; ik·'stingkt) No longer in existence.

During the Ice Age many animals became **extinct** because they couldn't live in the cold.

fossil (fos sil; 'fos·əl) The remains of a plant or animal of an earlier age. These remains have hardened and are preserved in earth or rock.

While sifting through the flakes of rock, Maria found a **fossil.**

harpoon (har poon; här·'po͞on) A pointed and barbed weapon with a rope attached. It is used to spear whales or large fish.

No **harpoon** would stay in the soft flesh of the large fish.

manatee (man a tee; 'man·ə·'tē) A slow-moving, clumsy animal that lives off the coast of Florida. It has flippers and a broad, flat tail.

The **manatee** floated near the shore, feeding on seaweed.

mermaid (mer maid; 'mûr·mād) An imaginary sea creature. It has the head and upper body of a woman and the tail of a fish.

The sailor said that he saw a **mermaid** sitting on a rock.

merman (mer man; 'mûr·man) An imaginary sea creature. It has the head and upper body of a man and the tail of a fish.

The **merman** flicked his tail and disappeared in a swirl of foam.

octopus (oc to pus; 'ok·tə·pəs) A sea animal with a large round head and eight long arms.

The fishers stared in horror as the giant **octopus** wound its arms around the boat.

Oiso (Oi so; öi·'sō) A resort town on the coast of Japan.

Many Japanese people vacation at **Oiso.**

paramedic (par a med ic; 'pâr·ə·med·ik) A person trained to give first aid to injured people.

The **paramedic** put the woman's leg in a splint.

sonar (so nar; 'sō·när) An instrument that locates underwater objects. It sends out sound waves and picks up their echoes.

By using **sonar,** scientists have discovered a large animal in Loch Ness.

squid (skwid) A sea animal with a long body, tail fins, and ten arms around its mouth.

The body of the giant **squid** was so soft that a rope cut right through it.

tentacle (ten ta cle; 'ten·tə·kəl) A long outgrowth from the body of an animal such as an octopus or squid. It is used for moving and for catching food.

Suddenly the sailors saw a huge **tentacle** come out of the water.

tidal wave (tid al wave; 'tīd·(ə)l wāv) A huge wave that sometimes follows an earthquake. It can go far inland and sweep people and houses out to sea.

When they heard that a **tidal wave** was coming, the people near the sea went to high ground.

tornado (tor na do; tôr·'nā·dō) A whirling wind that forms a funnel-shaped cloud. It moves in a narrow path near the ground.

The **tornado** picked up a row of houses and carried them a long way.

Yerkes Primate Center (Yer kes Pri mate Cen ter; 'yər·kēs 'prī·māt 'sen·tər) A place in Atlanta, Georgia where scientists work with apes.

Scientists trained Lana to "speak" at the **Yerkes Primate Center.**

Yerkish (Yer kish; 'yər·kish) A language using symbols instead of words.

Lana put symbols together to make up a sentence in **Yerkish.**

Other Books to Read

The colored dots tell you how easy or hard each book is to read.

● easy   ● average   ● hard

Disaster in Tokyo

● Gwynneth Ashby, <u>Looking at Japan</u>.
What would it be like to live in Japan? You can find out by looking at dozens of photographs as well as by reading about what they show.

● Jeannette Bruce, <u>Judo: A Gentle Beginning</u>.
Why are so many people turning to the fighting arts of Japan? This book will tell you.

● Lensey Namioka, <u>White Serpent Castle</u>.
The two young samurai were fighters who needed a job. Mystery, murder, and a ghost were waiting for them at White Serpent Castle.

Animal Talk

● Arthur C. Clarke, <u>Dolphin Island</u>.
Why did the dolphins save Johnny's life? Dr. Kazan thought he knew. For years he had been trying to talk with dolphins. Now dolphins were trying to get in touch with people.

● Helen Kay, <u>Apes</u>.
Can apes use and make tools? Can they paint pictures? Can they learn to talk with people? Here is what scientists are finding out.

- Konrad Lorenz, King Solomon's Ring.
  Solomon, the stories say, could talk with
  animals. In this book a famous scientist tells
  how he too learned the secrets of animal
  language. He did it by bringing wild creatures
  into his house.

The Blizzard

- Desmond Bagley, The Snow Tiger.
  McGill warned them that an avalanche would
  bury the town. They believed him—but it was
  already too late.

- B. Bartos-Hoppner, Avalanche Dog.
  Every weekend at the ski hut the boys took
  turns being buried under deep snow. Their dogs
  found them all right. Then came the killer
  avalanche that put the dogs to the real test.

- Laura Ingalls Wilder, The Long Winter.
  A blizzard struck in October. As the snow kept
  falling, the small pioneer town was cut off from
  the world. Somehow Laura knew that her
  family would survive.

Creatures of the Deep

- Jeanne Bendick, The Mystery of the Loch Ness
  Monster.
  Many scientists now believe that some large,
  unknown animal is living in Loch Ness. Here are
  the best guesses and the latest proofs.

Walter Beuhr, <u>Sea Monsters</u>.
Many monsters have come from the sea. Some are real, some aren't, and a few we still aren't sure about. This book ranges from prehistoric sea monsters to the Loch Ness monster of today.

Geoffrey Household, <u>The Spanish Cave</u>.
What huge monster lurked in the Spanish cave? There was only one way to find out.

F
G   5
H   6
I   7
J   8